Screw the BS:

How to Invest in Gold and Silver

By Tony Chou

Table of Contents

Part 3: How to Trade Gold and Silver

I dedicate this book to everyone who has helped me throughout my life.

This book was last updated in the summer of 2014.

I am not a gold bug who believes that gold and silver prices will go up forever. In fact, over the long term (i.e. 50 years) gold and silver do not retain their value when adjusted for inflation! Fortunately, no one invests with a 50 year time frame. 99% of investors want to buy and hold assets for a few years before selling them for handsome profits.

Fortunately, the opportunity of a decade is waltzing in front of us right now. Gold and silver prices will soar past their all time highs ($1900 for gold and $50 for silver) before this decade is over. Hence, precious metals investors will make far more profits than U.S. equities investors. Investors and traders must understand what gold and silver prices will do in the next few years so that they can profit handsomely from this long term (i.e. 20 years) bull market.

I wrote this book so that you can take advantage of this once-in-a-decade opportunity. What's in it for me? All the money that I make from books sales will be plowed back into my trading account, which owns a lot of gold and silver. I don't tell others to do one thing while I do something else.

This is not a get-rich-quick book. In the financial markets (including the gold and silver markets), it takes money to make money. Don't expect to buy $50 worth of silver, sit back for 3 years and watch that $50 turn into $5,000,000. If you invest or trade properly, $5,000 can turn into $50,000 in just a few years.

Before you read this book or buy it (if you haven't already), I'd like to tell you a little bit about me. I want you to make an informed decision as to whether this book is worth your time and money or not.

Disclaimer: I am not affiliated with dealers that sell gold and silver. I am merely a gold and silver trader who truly believes in the factors that are driving this long term bull market.

My Background

As a gold and silver trader, I spend hours each day analyzing gold and silver prices. My analysis is split into 2 sections: a long term analysis (3-5 year cycle) and a medium term analysis (3 months – 1 year cycle). I allude to both analyses in this book.

Trading for a couple of years, I have been pretty successful thus far. I have touched everything under the sun that's related to gold and silver investing. Today, I primarily trade gold and silver financial products. Thus I know a lot about gold and silver investing, because investing is the same as trading except with a longer time frame.

This book is split into 3 parts.

Part 1 discusses my long term prediction for gold and silver prices. This part draws on my years of analysis in the gold, silver, and commodities markets. A lot of investors do not pay enough attention to the big picture. They want to buy and hold gold and silver forever (or at least until they retire) without thinking. On the contrary, it is imperative that investors understand why gold and silver are in long term bull markets. Only by understanding the factors that drive this bull market can you predict when this bull market will end and when you should sell your gold or silver. Although Part 1 does include some terminology, I have simplified it as much as possible. Please do not skip this section of the book.

Part 2 teaches you how to invest in gold and silver without getting ripped off. This section is ideal for those who are keen on buying gold and silver but don't know where to begin. The longest section in this book, Part 2 explores all the possible options when it comes to investing in the precious metals markets.

Part 3 is for readers who want to trade gold and silver. Trading precious metals is very different from trading stocks and currencies. To aid your venture, I have divulged as much information as I can about trading precious metals without giving away any proprietary information.

In essence, this no-frills book keeps the BS to a minimum. 3…2…1… here we go!

Part 1

1. What Impact Gold and Silver Prices

Many investors do not know what factors cause gold and silver prices to go up or down. Let's first look at the factors that do not cause precious metals prices to rise.

Many people believe that gold and silver are safety havens during economic crises. They reason that everyone rushes to the "safety" of the precious metals market when stocks crash, thereby driving up gold and silver prices. This notion is totally false. Although gold and silver prices peaked half a year after U.S. stock prices peaked in 2007, precious metals prices eventually declined more than U.S. stock prices. Silver's price fell by 70% and gold's price fell by 40%. Why do precious metals prices fall when U.S. stock prices fall? It's the opposite of the maxim "a rising tide lifts all boats". In this scenario, a tsunami sinks all boats. Investors must dump everything to raise cash so that they can survive crises. Neither gold nor silver is a safety haven in times of crisis.

This is a gold chart during the 2008 financial crisis.

This is a silver chart during the 2008 financial crisis.

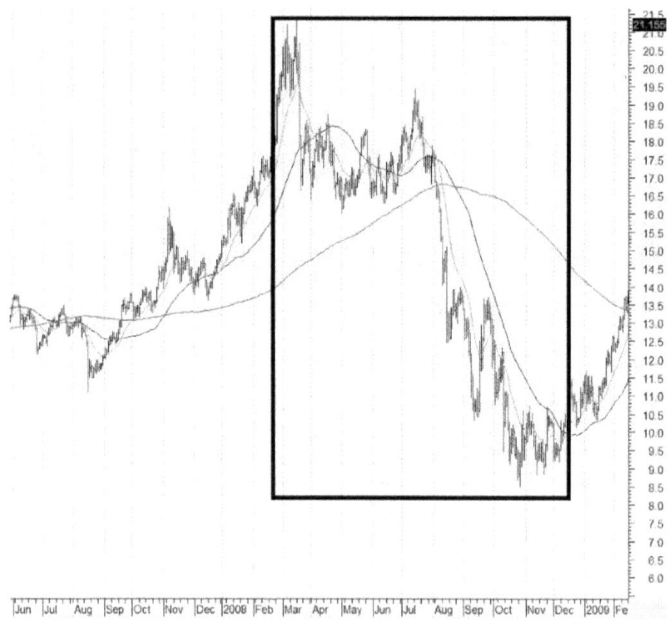

This misconception arises from the 1970s, when U.S. stocks languished for a decade while precious metals prices soared. In reality, gold and silver prices didn't rise because of the mediocre U.S. economy in the 1970s. Precious metals prices increased because of the 1970s' high inflation, which causes gold and silver prices to rise in the long term.

The second most common misconception regarding precious metals is that gold and silver supplies impact prices. This belief is incorrect. This quote from Hedge Fund Market Wizards reflects reality:

"Gold [and silver] are worth exactly what people think they're worth. Gold [and silver] are the only commodities (raw materials) whose amount of supply is literally a hundred times as much as the amount physically used in any year. This isn't true of any other commodity such as oil or corn, where totally supply and annual consumption demand are much closer in balance, and true shortages can develop. There is never any shortage of gold [or silver]. Therefore gold's and silver's values are entirely dependent on investor psychology or the fundamental factors that drive investor psychology. It's ridiculous how other analysts write long reports on gold and silver analyzing things like annual production and jewelry usage. Annual production and consumption of precious metals are only a very small fraction of supply, maybe around 1%, so who cares how much they change. The supply of precious metals has nothing to do with precious metals prices."

I couldn't have said it better myself. Gold and silver are mostly bought by investors and speculators. It is estimated that all the gold ever mined (the existing supply) is 158,000 tonnes, while the annual production of gold (additional supply) is merely 2,500 tonnes. The marginal new supply of gold hardly impacts the existing supply.

A tiny 2,000 tonnes goes towards industrial production and jewelry usages each year. Thus the majority of the demand comes from investors and speculators. As you can see, supply and industrial demand are insignificant when compared to the total supply and demand of gold.

Although silver does have a few more industrial uses than gold, the majority of silver's "demand" comes from traders. The silver market is smaller than the gold market and can be more easily manipulated. That is why many profit seeking traders prefer to trade silver than gold.

Now let's look at the two factors that cause precious metals prices to rise.

Factor #1 is the supply and demand for commodities that have practical applications, such as oil, copper, corn, wheat, natural gas, etc. Commodities with practical applications account for 99% of the commodities market. Meanwhile, gold and silver are commodities for which the demand from practical applications is tiny in comparison to the demand from investors and speculators. Rising demand for commodities that have practical applications results in rising commodity prices as a whole. Since a rising tide lifts all boats, gold and silver prices increase as well.

Connected to Factor #1, Factor #2 is inflation. Inflation means that paper money is worth less and consumers get less bang for their buck. Every country faces either deflation (negative inflation), little inflation, or high inflation. Deflation – a decrease in the general price of goods and services – is virtually nonexistent today. Deflation does not cause gold and silver prices to rise. On the contrary, it's high inflation that causes precious metals prices to go up. Spotting high inflation, investors have less faith in the U.S. dollar and rush to buy assets that they believe will attain their value in inflationary periods e.g. gold and silver. Subsequently, speculators and traders jump on the precious metals market, and soon prices are pushed sky-high.

Some "gurus" dispute the fact that inflation drives up precious metals prices. For example, Harvard Professor Martin Feldstein once wrote:

"Reconsider the potential of gold as a hedge against inflation. The average price of gold in 1980 was $400 (excluding the bubble's peak of $850). Ten years later, the U.S. CPI (inflation indicator) was up more than 60%, but the price of gold had not risen at all over those 10 years! And by the year 2000, the U.S. CPI was more than twice its level in 1980 while gold had FALLEN to $300 an ounce!"

The reality is that the gold and silver prices do not move in sync with inflation. Just because inflation is 3% doesn't mean that precious metals prices will rise 3%. When inflation is normal and negligible, gold and silver investors do not pay attention to it and thus inflation has no impact on gold and silver prices. This is why gold's price action was essentially flat from 1980 to 2000 despite inflation rising slowly at 3-4% per year.

Gold and silver prices only respond to red-hot inflation. Only when inflation is high and noticeable do investors rush to buy precious metals and drive prices up. This is why gold and silver prices soared in the late 1970s: the U.S. experienced consecutive years of 10%+ inflation.

When considering U.S. inflation, you must also consider U.S. interest rates. More accurately speaking, gold and silver prices correspond to the different between inflation and interest rates. The most widely watched interest rate is the Federal Funds Rate, set by the Federal Reserve (U.S. central bank). The Fed (short-form for Federal Reserve) changes the interest rate to:

1 – Stimulate a weak U.S. economy or cool a hot U.S. economy.

2 – Control U.S. inflation by raising interest rates successively.

Inflation always precedes significant increases in the Federal Funds Rate. Only when inflation becomes out of control does the Federal Reserve increase interest rates significantly. Why?

Raising interest rates significantly is like amputating the leg of a wounded patient. The short term pain is significant but the long term pain is obvious. Politicians being politicians (I'm talking to you, Congress!), short term pain is preferred over long term pain UNTIL the long term pain can no longer be ignored. Successive interest rate hikes kill the economy in the short term because businesses can't fund their operating costs. However, raising interest rates is beneficial in the long term because inflation is inevitably dangerous.

Only when inflation is too big to ignore do Federal Reserve officials have the political will to raise interest rates, crush the U.S. economy in the short term, and kill inflation.

For example, the 1970s was characterized by a weak economy and high inflation. Getting out of control, U.S. inflation reached 11.3% in 1979. A man with some serious balls, Federal Reserve Chairman Paul Volcker raised the Federal Funds Rate from 11.2% in 1979 to 20% in June 1981. Due to Volcker's valiant actions, inflation eventually peaked at 13.6% in 1981 and crashed to 3.2% in 1983.

Of course Volcker is praised as a hero today, but he was attacked left right and center by other politicians in 1980 (welcome to Washington).

Central banks buy and sell gold, not silver. The buying and selling of gold by central banks influences gold's price in the short term. Central banks generally do not announce their purchases in advance, so it's practically impossible to predict what they plan on doing. In addition, most central banks buy and sell gold from each other. This prevents a large seller from crashing the gold market or a large buyer from causing the price of gold to spike. Thus, their actions do not significantly alter gold's spot price.

2. The Current Bull Markets in Gold and Silver

Gold and silver prices were in long term bear markets from 1983 to 2001. Prices were essentially stagnant during this period (see the following chart for gold's price).

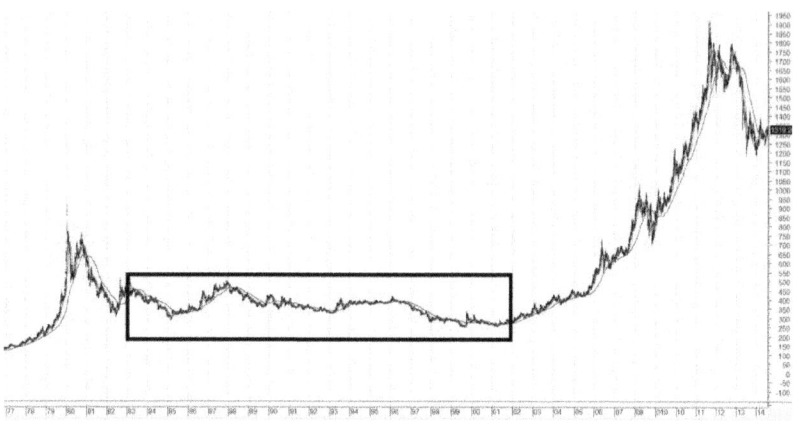

Gold and silver (and commodities in general) entered long term bull markets since 2001 that exist to this day. What factor resulted in a bear to bull market change in 2001?

Factor #1 (demand increases vastly and outstrips supply) took off like a rocket at the turn of the millennium. As of 2014, Factor #1 (inflation increases) has occurred while Factor #2 has yet to transpire.

Factor #1 did not exist in the 20th century. Many countries in Africa, South America, and Asia were rocked by political turmoil. As a result, the first world developed while the rest of the world was too economically trivial to consume vast amounts of resources. However, the poorer parts of the world began to develop by the 1980s. This economic development is exemplified by China, whose rise started to gain steam at the turn of the millennium. With the rise of developing nations, a lot more natural resources are being consumed than before.

Throughout history, increased demand has always been offset by increased supply from two sources: new lands with more natural resources and new technologies for extracting resources more efficiently. These two factors - new resources and new technology – have resulted in cheap commodity prices over the past 200 years. However, the world has reached a tipping point at which this 200 year commodity price decline (when adjusted for inflation) must reverse course. There is almost no untapped resource basins left and technology can only do so much. Technology is not limitless - it is constrained by the actual amount of natural resources, regardless of how efficiently we extract these resources.

This quote by legendary hedge fund manager Jeremy Grantham discusses why natural resource and agricultural supplies are dwindling.

"Agricultural progress is by nature arithmetic. If endless compound growth were possible, then eventually a single corn plant would have to produce a ton of food, or, in human terms, 6-foot tall women would one day be 40 feet tall. Each species has a limit that tends to be approached at a decelerating rate. In mathematical terms, this is known as an asymptote. A group of researchers looked at all of the important grain-producing areas – wheat and corn in the Midwest, wheat in Ukraine and Australia, rice in Japan and Thailand, corn in Brazil, and so on. They studied the change in productivity year by year. They concluded that not a single one could be described in exponential (or compound) terms. At best they had a steadily declining percentage gain or a linear increase. Even less encouragingly, many grain areas were best described as asymptotic to zero: that is, clearly heading eventually toward zero. Thomas Malthus predicted 200 years ago that agricultural productivity growth would steadily decline. So, how come we aren't all starving? Well, we had not one, but two, non-repeatable windfalls. First, there was new land. Malthus had no idea that west of the Mississippi, in Australia, and in parts of South America there were vast new

agricultural lands to exploit. Second, there was a realization that adding more nitrogen, potassium, and phosphorus could remarkably increase output, especially in the depleted soils of Europe and Asia, coupled with the discoveries of how to make nitrogen fertilizer and where to mine potassium and phosphorus. The use of fertilizer since 1950 more than quintupled per acre but today often reaches limits beyond which production actually falls. The increased use of fertilizer is also unsustainable in that environmental damage is often severe and the mined resources are, of course, depleting. In recent decades, despite the increased use of genetically modified crops and related technologies and continued progress in more traditional plant breeding, the growth rate in the productivity of grains is steadily declining."

Oil is an example of demand outstripping supply. For nearly a century, oil was cheap (around $17 a barrel) as new reserves were being discovered all the time. Demand suddenly outstripped supply in 1971 and oil prices shot through the roof. The new "normal" became $35 a barrel. By the 21st century, developing countries started to consume more oil. In 2005, demand further increased while supply languished, and the new "normal" became $80 a barrel.

Commodities have been in a long term bull markets since 2002 because demand continues to grow while supply is restrained by limited resources. Since a rising tide lifts all boats, all commodity prices – including that of gold and silver - have soared since 2002.

Factor #1 (demand outstripping supply) has been mostly played out by now. With her infrastructure mostly built, China has an overcapacity problem. Thus demand for commodities won't rise as fast as it did in the 21st century's first decade. If this long term bull market is to continue, it must be driven by a Factor #2: inflation must increase. Here's some background on U.S. inflation right now.

The Consumer Price Index (CPI) is the official measure of inflation. According to these statistics, U.S. inflation is very low as of summer 2014. This is weird because the U.S. government and other governments around the world have been printing tons of money to support their economies since the 2008 Great Recession. Historically speaking, every country that printed massive amounts of money experienced hyperinflation. Examples include Germany in the 1920s and France in the late 1700s. Never before has printing money solved a nation's economic woes without resulting in high inflation.

Anyone who's been grocery shopping recently knows that inflation is in fact very high. Meat, vegetables, and other raw material prices have doubled over the past year. It's only a matter of time before "official" inflation statistics reflect the real rate of inflation.

When inflation gallops away in the next few years, gold and silver prices will soar because these precious metals are seen as hedges against inflation (assets that retain their value in the face of inflation).

Don't expect the Federal Reserve to increase interest rates significantly when inflation rears its ugly head at first. With a weak U.S. economy and political deadlock, the Federal Reserve will only raise interest rates AFTER inflation has gotten out of control. Kicking the can down the road – that's what Washington D.C. does best.

3. The Future for Gold and Silver Prices

Looking at gold and silver charts, you can see that gold fell from a high of $1900 to a low of $1180 while silver fell from a high of $50 to a low of $18 an ounce. Does this massive price decline mean that the long term bull markets in precious metals are over? Of course not!

Based on my analysis, gold's final bottom should be around $1100, while silver's final bottom should be around $16. This means that gold and silver prices will make new bottoms before soaring to through the stratosphere.

There is a really famous investor that I respect, and he echoes my prediction regarding gold and silver prices making new bottoms before rising. With a great track record, Jim Rogers predicts that the final bottom for gold will occur in one year (approximately 2015) before precious metals prices start to rise. Jim Roger's reasons are simple – after a huge spike in 2010 and 2011, the price of gold needs to decline 40-50% from its $1900 peak before it starts to rise again and make a new all time high. Every mini-bubble in history was followed by a 40-50% price decline.

Jim Rogers' 2015 time target makes sense. In order for gold and silver prices to bottom from their multi-year declines since 2011, inflation must pick up. As of today (summer 2014), inflation has yet to increase drastically, which means that gold and silver prices aren't ready to rise yet. Fortunately, a prolonged period of high inflation is not in the distant future.

Many commodities and commodity sectors have already touched their multi-year bottoms. Commodities are split into 4 sectors: agriculture, energy, industrial metals, and precious metals. Out of these 4 sectors, 2 sectors have already hit rock bottom. Energy prices, as exemplified by the price of oil, touched bottom in the 2nd half of 2012. Agriculture touched bottom in January 2014. It is now only a matter of time (i.e. 1 year) before the metals markets touch bottom as well.

I believe that gold and silver prices will peak before this decade is over. It's worth noting that throughout history, the final ascent in any long term bull market does not take a long time to complete. Here's a simple analogy. It takes a long time to build and fuel a rocket. But it only takes a few minutes for the rocket to take off. Likewise, the final spikes in gold and silver prices will be in the near future - approximately 2017 or 2018.

However, it is important to remember that no one can predict at what price the market will peak. As a rule of thumb, I do know that all bull markets must exceed their previous all time highs by multiples. That is the characteristic of all bubbles (the final stage of a long term bull market) – the price at the peak is unimaginably high. This means that silver will vastly exceed $50 and gold will vastly exceed $1900.

Part 2

1. Terms You Need to Know

Before we look at various ways to buy gold and silver, here are some terms that you should understand.

Spot Price: The spot price is the price that's quoted on international gold and silver markets across the globe. Think of the spot price as the "official price" around the world. The spot price is what mints, central banks, and large institutional investors pay for massive quantities of physical gold or silver. Small investors (e.g. people with less than $5 million) must pay more than the spot price. Since the spot price is like the wholesale price, small investors must pay the retail price.

Premium: The premium is the additional price that small investors pay above the spot price. If the spot price for silver is $20 an ounce and the small investor paid $23, he/she paid a $3 premium. Premiums cover the costs of advertising precious metals, distributing and shipping the precious metals, and selling the metals via dealers. Unlike the spot price, there is no standard premium that everyone pays. Premiums range between 3%-20% spot price. There are some general guidelines for premiums.

1 – Larger gold/silver bars command smaller premiums because it's cheaper to market, ship, and sell larger bars (percentage-wise) than it is to sell smaller bars. It's is for the same reason why goods at Costco tend to be cheaper than goods at Wal-Mart.

2 – Premiums vary by mints. Mints that command higher premiums can do so because their coins are more desirable. Generally speaking, bullion that was refined by a federal mint (e.g. the U.S. Mint, the Canadian Mint) commands a higher premium than bullion that's refined by a private mint.

3. Premiums change with the fluctuations in gold and silver prices. When the spot price is falling very quickly, dealers want to sell their inventory and avoid the price decline. Thus they'll lower the premium to attract more buyers. When the spot price is soaring, dealers want to sell their inventory at a better price in the future. Thus they'll raise the premium to temporarily discourage buyers.

Troy ounces: The gold or silver price that you hear about on the news is the spot price for one ounce of gold or silver. A troy ounce – equivalent to 31.1 grams - is the global measurement unit for gold and silver.

Bullion: Physical gold and silver ("physical" means you can actually touch) are found in many shapes and forms. Bullion is gold or silver that's in the shape of a bar. Each bullion bar is stamped with the name of the mint that refined it, the bar's weight (typically in ounces), and the purity (what percent of the bar is actually gold or silver). Although most mints refine bullion to 0.999 purity, the Canadian mint refines to 0.9999 purity.

Junk: Over 50 years ago, mints around the world used some gold and silver in their coins. These are called junk coins, and today their value is based on their gold or silver contents. Mints discontinued using gold and silver in their coins in the 1960s. Since many individuals looked for junk coins in their pocket change during the 1970s (when precious metals prices were high), there are very few junk coins left in circulation.

Weights: Silver and gold bullion come in many different weights. Typical weights are one ounce, ten ounce, and a hundred ounce bars. Heavier bars command lower premiums (percentage-wise) because mints can spend less money on cutting the precious metals into smaller pieces. 100 grams and 1 kilogram bullion does exist, and they are mostly minted by the Canadian mint. Avoid investing in bullion that's weighted in the metric system because the global markets for gold and silver are based on the troy ounce system.

In the next few chapters we'll look at the different forms of gold and silver that you can invest in.

2. Invest in Gold or Silver Bullion

In the past, the most popular way to invest in gold and silver was to buy gold and silver bars, also known as bullion. But with the invention of ETFs (which I'll discuss in a later chapter), bullion has decreased significantly in popularity due to its many drawbacks.

The main disadvantage of buying bullion is that you pay more than the spot price. Your goal as a gold or silver investor is to buy/sell at a price that's as close to the spot price as possible. After all, no one likes to pay dealers a higher premium than he/she has to or sell to dealers at a lower price than he/she has to.

With that being said, here is everything you need to know about buying and selling gold and silver bullion.

There are 3 places to buy gold and silver bullion.

1 – A coin and bullion store

2 – A coin and bullion store's online presence

3 – An online-only dealer

You can physically buy gold and silver bullion from coin and bullion stores. These dealers charge the highest premiums. After sampling 2 stores per state (total of 100 stores), I found that the average premium is 17%. In other words, the instant you buy physical gold or silver from these stores, you've lost 17% of your money. Not very appealing, is it?

However, buying from these stores is relatively hassle-free. You simply walk into the store any time you want, tell the clerk you want to buy X amounts of gold or silver, show them your passport and a piece of photo ID (you need to prove that you're an American citizen – this is for "anti-terrorist" purposes), and pay the spot price + premium. You cannot use your credit card to pay – credit cards charge merchants more than 3%. Since dealers only apply a 17% markup, the 3% credit card fee is too much to bear. Hence, dealers require you to pay with cash or debit. If you're going to buy in-store, please only buy from reputable dealers. In Canada and the U.S.A., dealers have to be registered with the federal government. Please do not buy from unlicensed dealers, which are probably scams.

Alternatively, many coin & bullion stores have websites where you can purchase gold or silver and pick up your purchase in-store within 5 business days. After sampling 2 stores per state (total of 100 stores), I found that the average premium is 10%. Why do the same dealers charge you less when you buy online than when you buy in-store? The reason is simple.

When you buy in-store, the dealer is paying for expensive retail space. When you pre-order, dealers can store that gold/silver in a cheap distant warehouse until you pickup you're order. Thus, dealers' overhead costs are lower because they can rent smaller storefronts. This is why it's cheaper to buy goods on Amazon than it is to buy goods at your local superstore.

This is how buying gold and silver online works, from my personal experience. You (the customer) go to the dealer's website and checkout with an order to buy X amounts of gold/silver at the spot price + the 10% premium. Instead of paying online, you enter your credit card and pay a $10 deposit. Within five business days you must pickup your gold/silver in-store and pay with cash, debit card or bank draft (many stores don't accept cheques due to prevalent cheque frauds in recent years). Since you already paid a $10 deposit, the dealer will deduct $10 from your purchase total. If, you fail to pick up your gold/silver within 5 business days, the dealer keeps the $10 deposit.

Lastly, the cheapest way to buy physical gold or silver is to buy from a website that has no physical store. One of the largest online-only retailers of gold/silver bullion is APMEX (disclaimer: I have no affiliation with them). These e-retailers typically charge 5% premiums plus flat shipping and handling fees (which can easily amount to a total of a 7% premium). You don't need to worry about shipments getting lost in the mail because online retailers buy insurance from UPS and FedEx. If you're going to buy online, only buy from the largest e-retailers. It's too easy to get scammed online due to the inability to examine the goods before paying.

Unscrupulous dealers may sell you a gold "bar" that's actually copper on the inside and plated with a thin layer of gold. Real gold is very heavy relative to its size.

Out of these 3 options, buying from an online-only dealer is the cheapest way to invest in gold and silver. Even after factoring in shipping costs, buying online is still significantly cheaper than buying from the other two options.

It's worth mentioning that many in-store retailers and online retailers lower their premiums if you buy in bulk. However, these bulk discounts aren't significant. For example, if you buy 1 ounce of gold, the dealer might charge a 17% markup. If you buy 10 ounces, they might charge a 15% markup. If you buy 100 ounces, they might charge a 14% markup. Regardless of how much you buy, the dealer will still charge a hefty premium.

Gold and silver bullion is categorized by purity. "Purity" refers to how well refined the metal is. Gold that's stamped ".999" means that for every 1000 parts of that "gold" bar, 999 parts are gold and 1 part is a non-gold metal. It is impossible to have 100% gold as technology does not allow refineries to be that precise.

Many mints produce different bullion purities. For example, the Royal Canadian Mint is world renown for producing some of the finest bullion and coins in the world - .9999 bullion and higher. The global standard, on the other hand, is .999 and is widely adopted by nations like the U.S.A. Each piece of bullion is engraved with its purity.

As an investor, I recommend that you only invest in .999 gold and silver because that is the global standard. When the media reports "gold is currently trading at $1600 an ounce", it is referring to .999 gold. There is no standard market price for any other purity of gold or silver. Thus, it makes sense to invest in the only purity that has a standard market price – .999 gold and silver.

There are many mints (both government and private) that refine bullion. It really doesn't matter which mint the bullion comes from, as long as:

1 - The bullion is of .999 purity, as discussed above. Some mints only produce .9999 bullion, like the Canadian Mint.

2 – The bullion's price is as close to the spot price as possible. You don't want to pay excessively high premiums. Mints charge different prices because of slightly varying costs.

Basically, the idea is simple. You want to buy .999 gold or silver from a reputable dealer that charges the lowest premium.

When the precious metals bull markets peak, make sure that you sell your gold or silver to a legitimate coin and bullion store. Never sell your precious metals to a Cash For Gold company.

There are tons of problems with Cash For Gold companies:

1 – After melting down your precious metals, Cash For Gold companies pay ridiculously low sums for your gold and silver. If these companies can spend millions of dollars on ads, they must be paying you a lot less money for your gold and silver. Even pawn shops pay you more. According to an article by The Consumerist, "majority of the time customers are outraged when they lay eyes on the amount of their check. Some customers even receive checks for $0.01".

2 – Cash For Gold companies say that you can return your check if you're not satisfied with the amount. However, there are many restrictions that will inhibit you from doing so, even if the size of your check is ridiculously small. It's all in the fine print.

3 – Many Cash For Gold companies are under federal investigation for securities fraud and money laundering for terrorist organizations.

Legitimate coin and bullion stores do not have these problems. Going in to sell your gold or silver, an employee will immediately give you a quote before conducting the transaction. Generally speaking, the store will pay you 5% below the spot price, which is a pretty good deal. If you agree to the price, the store will complete the transaction by paying you in cash. Everything is conducted in a fair and square manner within a matter of minutes. There is no chicanery or crooked dealing.

3. Invest in Gold or Silver Coins

There are 2 types of coins: bullion-like coins and numismatic coins.

Bullion-like Coins

These are essentially just gold or silver bullion that are minted into the shape of a coin with a simplistic engraving on them. Bullion-like coins are generally made by national mints like the U.S. or Canadian Mint. Other prominent government mints include those of China, South Africa, Australia, Austria, and Mexico.

The U.S. Mint mints "American Silver Eagles" and "American Gold Eagles". Each Silver Eagle weighs 1 ounce and is composed of 0.999% silver. Each Gold Eagle weighs 1.0909 ounces and is composed of 91.67% gold, 3% silver, and 5.33% copper (the gold content is still 1 ounce – the silver and copper contents make the coin less malleable). Both Silver and Gold Eagles are engraved with an image of Lady Liberty on one side and an American eagle on the other side.

The prices of Silver and Gold Eagles are typically the same as that of silver or gold bullion. This means that a 1 ounce silver or gold eagle typically costs 10-15% more than the spot price for gold or silver. Each year, the U.S. Mint roles out new sets of Silver or Gold Eagles, the only difference being the updated year that's engraved on the coin. Below is an image of an American Gold Eagle.

On a side note, I'd like to mention that some Silver and Gold Eagles that are in excellent condition have numismatic value. Coin collectors value these Silver and Gold Eagles, which command higher premiums than normal Silver and Gold Eagles. When buying Silver or Gold Eagles from the Mint or a dealer, you'll receive Eagles that are in great condition. However, if you want a flawless Eagle, the premium will be much higher (hence the numismatic value). As an investor (and not a coin collector), just buy the regular Silver or Gold Eagle.

The U.S. Mint has two other popular coins: the Gold Buffalo and the Silver Buffalo. The Gold Buffalo weighs 1 ounce and is 0.999 gold (no other metals mixed with it, unlike the American Gold Eagle). The Silver Buffalo also weighs 1 ounce and is 0.999 silver. Both coins have an American bison (buffalo) on one side and a Native American on the other side. This is what a Silver Buffalo looks like.

The Canadian Mint mints .9999 gold or silver "Maple Leafs". Premiums on these coins are typically higher than that of U.S. Silver or Gold Eagles due to the extra purity (the additional "9"). Avoid investing in these because the global market for gold and silver is based upon a .999 purity standard, not a .9999 purity standard. Below is an image of a Canadian Gold Maple Leaf.

Another thing I'd like to mention is that all coins minted by government mints are legal tender, meaning that you can legally use these gold or silver coins to purchase goods and services. However, there's a catch. The face values of these coins are far less than what the precious metals that they contain are worth. For example, 1 ounce Gold Eagles (worth $1300 on the market as of summer 2014) are engraved with face values of $50, making it highly unlikely that anyone will use these gold coins to purchase any items. Likewise, 1 ounce Silver Eagles (worth $20 on the market as of summer 2014) are engraved with face values of $1.

Rounds are bullion-like coins that are minted by private mints. Rounds are not of legal tender since they weren't minted by governments. Rounds generally command smaller premiums because they do not have the "official" backing of a government.

Numismatic Coins

Numismatic coins have either artistic, commemorative, or scarcity value and are treasured by coin collectors. Thus, their premiums are a lot higher than that of bullion or bullion-like coins. Many numismatic coins are pleasing to the eye, but as an investor, you should avoid these. Here's why:

1 – Numismatic coins command much higher premiums than bullion-like coins. Whereas the typical premium for physical gold or silver is 10-20%, coins with numismatic value have at least a 50% premium due to their popularity with coin collectors and their artistic value. Numismatic coins are like diamonds – their monetary values depreciate the moment they're sold.

2 - The investment returns don't stack up. If the price of gold increased by, for example, 20%, the value of a gold numismatic coin might only rise 8%. This is because a large chunk of the coin's value isn't based on the gold's price but on the coin's numismatic value. Only a small chunk of the coin's

value is based on the underlying gold price. As an investor, you should maximize your returns by buying gold or silver itself.

3 – It is very hard to sell your numismatic coins at a good price. There is no standard value for a numismatic coin. These coins are like fine art: "appraisals" are just wild guesses. The real price is whatever a few whimsical buyers are willing to pay. Unfortunately, you cannot sell your numismatic coins to dealers for a good price. Dealers buy numismatic coins at prices that are slightly above the value of the coins' gold/silver contents. For example, I bought a Chinese Silver Panda (1 ounce coin) for $48 when silver cost $30 an ounce. I subsequently asked the dealer how much they would pay if I sold the Silver Panda to him, and he replied "$31" – a mere $1 above the spot price. Hence a lot of numismatic coin owners sell their coins on eBay. This way they can turn as much of their paper profits into real profits.

4 – 97% of counterfeit coins are numismatic coins. Many old and rare coins are counterfeits because it's almost impossible for non-experts to discern between fakes and the real deal. Even experts can be fooled. For example, experts use a sophisticated technology to determine whether an ancient coin really was minted hundreds of years ago or not. However, a

man in Europe recently discovered that if you walked through an airport security checkpoint many times with a coin in your pocket, the coin's surface will change. This change allows the coin to fool this sophisticated technology.

Many numismatic coins are not .999 gold or silver – they mix multiple metals to create an artistic effect. Likewise, many numismatic coins have non-metallic components that lend to the artistic effect. For example, the Canadian Mint is renowned for embedding Swarovski crystals in their numismatic coins. Below is an example of a Canadian numismatic coin. Notice the blue sapphire on the coin. At the time of this writing, silver is currently $22 an ounce while this coin is $63 CAD. Even after factoring the almost 1:1 ratio between the USD and CAD, this coin still commands a large premium.

Numismatic coins are graded based on their perfection (or lack of). The two main coin grading companies in the U.S. are the NGC (Numismatic Guaranty Corporation) and the PCGS (Professional Coin Grading Service). PCGS coins are typically more expensive because buyers PERCEIVE PCGS to have stricter and more consistent grading standards. Whether this perception is true or false is up for debate. It doesn't really matter. NGC graded coins are also slightly more common than PCGS graded coins.

Both companies use the MS scale for grading. MS-70 (Mint State – 70) is the highest rating, meaning that a coin with this rating is of perfect condition. MS-69 is the second highest rating, MS-68 is the third highest rating, and so on. MS-70 coins command much higher premiums than MS-69 coins because there are always a few rich folks who are willing to pay astronomical amounts for perfect condition coins. For example, a 1990 China Silver Panda MS-68 costs $140 and a 1900 China Silver Panda MS-69 costs $170. A 1990 China Silver Panda MS-70 is astronomically more expensive - $260 a coin.

Some unscrupulous dealers lie that "governments can confiscate bullion and bullion-like coins, but can't confiscate numismatic coins." By doing so, these dealers want you to buy their numismatic coins, which are sold at the highest markups.

Yes, it is true that the U.S. government confiscate gold bullion and bullion-like coins in 1933. President Roosevelt's Executive Order 6102 required U.S. citizens to exchange their gold for $20.67 per ounce (equivalent to $380 today). Coins with "special value to collectors of rare and unusual coins" were exempt from this order. The Gold Clause Act of 1934 nullified Executive Order 6102 and thus made it legal for citizens to own gold again in any form.

Are you afraid that a similar Executive Order may be issued in the future? Don't be. In reality, the government can confiscate anything in the name of "national security", including your gold, your business, your house, etc. All they have to do is stoke up enough public anger. Just ask the Japanese Americans whose properties were confiscated during WWII. Whether it's bullion or numismatic coins, Big Brother can take anything He wants to. Buying numismatic coins at insanely expensive premiums isn't going to save your ass when the government goes haywire. Thus I advise you to stick with bullion or bullion-like coins.

4. Invest in Gold or Silver ETF's

An ETF is the best way to invest in gold and silver. What is an ETF?

ETF stands for *exchange traded fund*. Essentially, it's an investment vehicle that allows you to invest in markets that you otherwise can't touch. You couldn't buy or sell gold/silver at the spot price before the invention of ETF's, unless you trade options and futures, which are complex financial products. Since trading options and futures takes a considerable amount of skill, most average investors couldn't buy gold and silver at the market price. Thus they had no option but to pay dealers hefty premiums.

But with invention of gold and silver ETFs, all of these problems were solved. The ETF **tries** to match the spot price for gold or silver as closely as possible. The ETF accomplishes this by buying/selling futures and options so that they can produce a "stock" (the ETF) that matches the underlying security's price as closely as possible. Each ETF has a ticker symbol, just like stocks do. For example, a silver ETF's ticker symbol is SLV. Thanks to ETF's you can buy gold and silver at prices close to the spot price without paying an inflated premium! This is especially attractive if you want to actively buy and sell gold/silver. Instead of dealers taking a 10% pound of flesh here, another 10% there, and another 10% here, a gold or silver ETF investor forgoes all these premiums and instead gets to buy or sell at a price close to the spot price.

However, notice that I said "the ETF **tries** to match the spot price for gold and silver as closely as possible." The key word here is "TRIES". There are many ETFs for gold and silver – some of them are so horribly managed that they track the spot price very poorly. We want to find and invest in the ETF that tracks the gold/silver spot price as closely as possible. Here's how to differentiate between a good ETF you should trade and a bad ETF you should stay away from:

1 - Volume. ETF's with more volume are better because they are liquid. Sometimes, an ETF with little volume will shut down, causing you (the investor) big problems. ETF's that shutdown will refund your money, but there's a ton of paperwork and hassle involved.

2 - Net assets. Avoid ETF's that have low net assets, which shows that the ETF is unpopular. The more popular an ETF is the better it will match the underlying market price (i.e. gold's

or silver's price). To find an ETF's net assets, just type in the ETF's ticker symbol on Google Finance.

3 - Correlation with the underlying security. ETF's that match the price actions of their respective underlying securities (e.g. SLV and silver) are better because the purpose of an ETF is to allow small investors to trade markets that they otherwise can't.

Now the question begs itself, how do you determine how well an ETF is correlated with its underlying security?

A simple Excel calculation will suffice. Set up a simple chart:

1 - Column 1: the underlying security itself: (price on Day 2) / (price on Day 1) – 1

2 - Column 2: the ETF: (price on Day 2) / (price on Day 1) – 1

Divide the results of Column 2 by Column 1. The result of this division should be 1 if the ETF properly matches its underlying market price.

For silver, **SLV** (iShares Silver Trust) is the best ETF because it is the most popular ETF and matches the silver spot price more closely than any other ETF. The price of one share of SLV is 1/10 of the price of one ounce of silver, but SLV's daily price fluctuations (percentage-wise) are the same as that of silver's.

For gold, the best ETF is **GLD** (SPDR Gold Trust) because it is the most liquid ETF and matches the gold spot price more closely than any other gold ETF. The price of one share of GLD is 1/10 of the price of one ounce of gold, but GLD's daily price fluctuations (percentage-wise) are the same as that of gold's.

It's worth noting that when you buy a gold or silver ETF, you cannot actually take delivery or touch the gold/silver. The company that manages your ETF sets aside gold or silver in a bank depository.

To rehash, investing in gold or silver ETF's has several advantages over investing in physical bullion or coins.

1 – You don't pay the excessive dealers' premiums.

2 – You're basically paying the spot price for your gold or silver. A well managed ETF will track the gold and silver with almost a 1:1 correlation.

3 - You can buy or sell at any time as long as the markets are open (Monday to Friday, 9:30 – 4). There is no lag between the time you decide to buy/sell and the time you actually sell (because if you're buying/selling physical silver, you'll have to drive to the dealer and waste time in a physical transaction).

Many doomsayers are scared that if the whole financial system and the U.S. dollar collapse, ETF's will become worthless pieces of paper. Thus, they say that you MUST buy physical gold and silver that you can touch and see with your own eyes.

The biggest problem with this belief is the underlying perception that gold/silver is "real wealth" which will save your ass when the world ends. Obviously this is not true. Gold and silver will be worth nothing when the world ends. You can't eat gold and silver and you can't use them for any real purposes (e.g. fashion bullets out of them). Sorry to break it to you, but when the financial system "implodes" and the whole world goes to hell, we as a human race are all going down together. Owning a couple of ounces of gold isn't going to save you and your family. When Rome besieged Jerusalem in 70 A.D., the price of a donkey head (food!) shot up by 35x in terms of gold and silver.

Before I conclude this chapter, I have a word of caution. Avoid ETN's like the plague. ETN's (Exchange Traded Note) are just like ETF's except that they're issued by banks. Your entire ETN investment will become worthless if the bank goes bankrupt. I'm not trying to scare you like those doomsayers – I've seen this happen. I have a friend who bought Lehman Brothers' ETN's during the 2008 Crash. The ETNs' values held steady in 2008. But the instant Lehman closed its doors, those ETNs went to zero (100% loss!). So I repeat: invest and trade ETF's, not ETN's. ETF's are managed by companies that specialize in the ETF business. The management companies are so insanely profitable that they never go bankrupt. After all, their business involves practically zero risk.

5. Do Not Invest in Gold or Silver Futures

Like ETF's, futures are financial products for investing or trading gold and silver. Futures employ massive leverage, resulting in massive losses and profits from relatively small price movements in the underlying market. Investors should definitely stay away from futures.

Futures can be very beneficial for traders because this leverage can maximize returns, if yielded properly. However, gold and silver futures have become increasingly unnecessary with the introduction of leveraged gold and silver ETF's. These leveraged ETF's can match the volatility of futures, which means that there's really no point in trading futures.

Gold and silver futures are primarily traded on the New York Commodities Exchange (COMEX) in the United States. Every futures contract has two sides. People buy futures contracts if they expect the price of gold or silver to go up. These people have "long" positions. On the contrary, people sell futures contracts if they expect the price of gold or silver to go down. These people have "short" positions.

The most commonly traded gold futures contract is GC. Each GC futures contract is for 100 ounces of gold. This "100" is called the "multiplier" in futures trading terminology. The most commonly traded silver futures contract is SI. Each SI futures contract is for either 1000 ounces or 5000 ounces of silver. Thus, each silver futures contract either has a 1000 multiplier or a 5000 multiplier.

The minimum that the price of gold or silver can fluctuate at any moment is $0.001 per ounce. Since a standard gold futures contract has a multiplier of 100, each $0.001 move in gold's price results in a $0.1 change in the price of the gold futures contract.

As I already mentioned, futures prices are volatile because they have leverage, also known as "margin". With gold (or silver) futures, you only pay a fraction of the cost of 100 ounces of gold when you buy 1 gold futures contract. For example a futures contract that contains 100 ounces of gold is worth $130,000 at the price of $1,300 per ounce. However, a single gold futures contract only costs $6,750, not $130,000. This $6,750 is known as the "initial margin". See how insanely leveraged a futures contract is? With an initial margin of $6,750 and the 100 ounces (multiplier) of gold being worth $130,000, you're leveraged by more than 19.25 times. This means that every $1 fluctuation in the price of gold or silver is equivalent to a $19.25 fluctuation in the value of your futures contract.

In addition to the initial margin, there is also something called the "maintenance margin". The maintenance margin is the price level at which your futures contract cannot fall to if you are to avoid a margin call. This is similar to a loss-limit. Right now (as of summer 2014) the maintenance margin for the gold futures contract GC is $5400. Every broker sets different margin requirements. Risk adverse brokers like mine set higher maintenance margin requirements, whereas more audacious brokers set lower maintenance margin requirements. If you face a margin call, your broker will give you two options:

A) Add more money into your brokerage account so that your account's value is once again above the maintenance margin threshold, or…

B) Sell some of your futures contracts at a loss and use that cash to meet the initial (not maintenance) margin requirements for your other futures contracts.

6. Invest in Gold or Silver Stocks

Another way to invest in the precious metals long term bull markets is to buy the stocks of gold and silver mining companies. My advice is to avoid doing so – mining companies are unattractive for four reasons.

1 – You're basically gambling on the mining company's ability to discover new gold/silver veins in the future. ("Veins" are bodies or gold or silver ore that are buried deep in the ground.) If the company can't find new gold/silver deposits, then it will probably go bankrupt because old veins will run out. As shrewd investors, we do not want to gamble. Even the company's management cannot accurately predict its ability to discover new gold and silver deposits.

2 – Just because gold or silver prices rise does not mean mining stocks will rise. The price of oil, a major cost for refineries and mining corporations, often rises when gold and silver prices rise. Thus, mining companies' costs rise along with rising revenue, resulting in stagnant profits and stagnant stock prices.

3 – Investing in gold or silver mining companies means that you have an extra layer of factors to worry about. If you're buying mining stocks because you expect precious metals prices to go up, then you should just invest in the precious metals outright. When you invest in a mining stock you have to worry about how good the company's management is, how well they manage their costs, etc. As investors, we want to make simple and clear decisions, which will lead to profitable investments.

4 – Many mining stocks are nothing more than scams. A mining stock is cheap when the company has yet to prove its gold or silver reserves. Many of those "massive gold and silver veins" reports are nothing more than shams that cheat investors of their money.

For reference sake, here's a list of the 8 largest gold companies in the world (ranked by market capitalization) and their return-on-investments since January 1, 2000 to February 20, 2013. All prices are in USD.

1 - Barrick Gold Corporation: + 70.14%

2 - Goldcorp Inc.: + 1025.91%

3 - Newmont Mining Corp: + 65.55%

4 - Newcrest Mining Limited: + 208.21%

5 - AngloGold Ashanti Limited: - 3.24%

6 - Yamana Gold Inc.: + 449.62%

7 - Kinross Gold Corporation: +32.62%

8 - Gold Fields Limited: + 127.53%

During this time, gold returned + 442.85%. As you can see, most of these gold companies underperformed the return-on-investment of gold itself. This list doesn't include a lot of the gold companies that went bankrupt. I don't mean to sound like a broken record, but investing in gold and silver stocks involves a lot of unnecessary risks. Just stick to directly investing in gold and silver.

Instead of buying and selling individual miner stocks, you can trade gold miner ETF's like GDX. Notice that I said "trade gold miner ETF's", not "invest in gold miner ETF's". This is because gold miners ETF's are very volatile, thus more suited for traders than investors. To maximize this volatility, most traders do not trade GDX, a non-leveraged ETF whose fluctuations are equal to that of gold's. Most miner traders trade NUGT, which is a 3x leveraged gold miner ETF (more volatility!).

NUGT is insanely volatile, which is why I stay away from this ETF. NUGT's price can easily spike or crash 30% on a reversal day!

Some foolish traders say "no problem – I can handle NUGT's short term volatility." NUGT has a structural problem – it erodes like crazy in the long term. Look at this 1 year chart (mid-2013 to mid-2014) for NUGT. NUGT literally gets crushed in the long term.

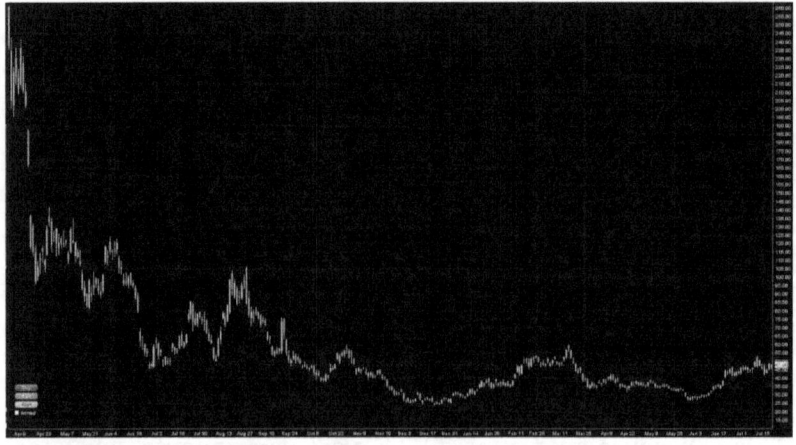

On April 2, 2013 NUGT traded at $250. NUGT currently (July 1, 2014) trades at $45. NUGT can only be used for trades that last a few days to a few weeks. Any long position in NUGT will get crushed over the course of a few months.

Since gold miners should be traded for no more than a few weeks, it is imperative that traders understand gold miners' correlations with other markets. Herein lies the problem. The prices of miner stocks are correlated U.S. equities (because gold miners are *stocks*) AND to gold's price (because they're *gold* miners). If the price of gold and U.S. equities move in opposite directions, it's hard to predict which one of these two markets gold miners will follow.

Many other factors that impact the prices of mining stocks are completely out of investors' and management's controls. Many gold and silver mines are located in politically unstable countries like Russia, Venezuela, and various African nations. Governments in these nations have "nationalized" (stolen) private mines in the past, leaving mining companies and their investors with big fat losses.

7. Do Not Buy Junk Silver

Junk silver refers to any coin that has no numismatic value and is only worth the amount of silver that it contains. Unlike bullion-like coins, junk silver coins are mostly 90% silver coins that were once in circulation (used in every day transactions). These coins included dollars, half dollars, quarters, dimes, and nickels. The U.S., Canadian, and many European governments actually used to use some silver in their coins, back in the day when silver was cheap. In 1965 the U.S. government stopped using silver in their coinage due to rising silver prices.

Today, the silver value in these coins is worth more than the coins' face values. None of these coins are 100% silver – all of them are a form of silver alloy. Here's a list of common coins in the U.S. that contain silver.

1 - All dimes minted before 1964 are of 90% silver. The value of the silver component (as of July 2014 market prices) is $1.50.

2 - All quarters minted before 1964 are of 90% silver. The value of the silver component (as of July 2014 market prices) is $3.75.

Most of the dimes and quarters minted before 1964 have already been pulled out of circulation and melted down by savvy businessmen.

However, many coin and bullion shops still sell "junk silver" at a price that's slightly lower than the value of the silver content. This is because it costs money to extract the 90% silver from the other metals.

As an investor, you should avoid investing in junk silver. You'd have to melt down and refine the junk silver in order for it to be worth anything. Refining is a really expensive and complicated business – it's simply not worth the time to buy junk silver and extract the silver components. The refinery costs may very well exceed any discounts that the dealer gives you for buying junk silver.

Below is a list of all the American junk silver coins available and the value of their silver contents, courtesy of Coinflation.com.

Description	Face Value	Silver Value
1942-1945 Nickel *	$0.05	$1.1663
1892-1916 Barber Dime	$0.10	$1.4995
1916-1945 Mercury Dime	$0.10	$1.4995
1946-1964 Roosevelt Dime	$0.10	$1.4995
1892-1916 Barber Quarter	$0.25	$3.7489
1916-1930 Standing Liberty Quarter	$0.25	$3.7489
1932-1964 Washington Quarter	$0.25	$3.7489
1892-1915 Barber Half Dollar	$0.50	$7.4979
1916-1947 Walking Liberty Half Dollar	$0.50	$7.4979
1948-1963 Franklin Half Dollar	$0.50	$7.4979
1964 Kennedy Half Dollar	$0.50	$7.4979
1965-1970 Half Dollar (40% silver)	$0.50	$3.0658
1878-1921 Morgan Dollar	$1.00	$16.0336
1921-1935 Peace Dollar	$1.00	$16.0336
1971-1976 Eisenhower Dollar (40% silver) **	$1.00	$6.5555
1986-2013 Silver Eagle (.999 Silver)	$1.00	$20.7092

Below is a list of all the Canadian junk silver coins available and the value of their silver contents.

Description	Face Value	Silver Value (USD)
1920-1967 Dime	$0.10	$1.2437
1967-1968 Dime (50% silver) **	$0.10	$.7773
1920-1967 Quarter	$0.25	$3.1094
1967-1968 Quarter (50% silver) **	$0.25	$1.9434
1920-1967 Half Dollar	$0.50	$6.2189
1935-1967 Dollar	$1.00	$12.4379

On a side note, "junk gold" does exist but is insanely rare. Most governments stopped using any gold in their coinage by the early 20th century – any coin that has gold in it probably has numismatic value.

8. Compare the Forms of Gold and Silver Investing

Out of all the forms of gold and silver investing that I've discussed, gold and silver ETF's are the most attractive. Some doomsayers say that ETF's are financial products and that all financial products will go to hell when the world ends. They say that the only thing you should buy is stuff that you can touch and keep under your mattress in case of an Armageddon (i.e. physical gold and silver).

Seriously, can we get over with the whole Armageddon scenario? Even if the world does end, physical gold and silver isn't going to help you. Gold and silver won't protect your family if the world ends – only a gun and a ton of food will. After all, you can't eat gold. The problem with buying physical gold and silver is that dealers charge a hefty premium and it costs money to store the gold and silver securely.

Gold and silver ETF's do not have these problems. These ETF's do not charge any premium besides a tiny 0.1% brokerage fee to buy and sell ETF's. In addition, there is no storage hassle when you invest in precious metals ETF's.

On the other hand, you should not invest in precious metals futures. As already mentioned, futures contracts are really complex financial instruments that will wipe out inexperienced traders in a heartbeat. Even many experienced traders avoid futures, whose leverage can be replicated by leveraged ETF's, which do not have the potential of margin calls.

9. Where to Store Physical Gold and Silver

There are many places where you can store your physical gold and silver.

Most banks rent safety deposit boxes where tenants can store their valuables, such as precious metals bars and coins. The fees associated with safety deposit boxes vary by the box's size. Boxes cost anywhere between $100 to $300 per year. As a general rule of thumb, a box that can hold 1 pound costs $1. The beauty about buying gold and silver is that you won't need a very large box unless you own millions of dollars worth of silver and gold. 10 pounds of gold is worth $156,000 at the price of $1300 an ounce.

Some people say that you should not store your gold and silver with a company that's connected to the financial system (i.e. banks). They say that you'll have problems recovering your gold and silver if the bank declares bankruptcy. On the contrary, banks are one of the best places to store your precious metals. If the bank fails, you will still get your gold and silver back. All that's required is a little more paperwork.

The possibility of a bank failure is the same as the possibility of other storage companies failing.

You can also store your gold and silver in a safe at home. You can buy fire-proof and water-proof safes for less than $200 on Amazon.com. If you intend on pursuing this option, please talk to your insurance agent. Gold and silver stored at home in safes are covered by the "Personal Articles Policy", which is not the same as the homeowner's policy. Your gold and silver can be insured if a thief breaks into your house and steals the safe along with its contents. If you plan on buying insurance, it's better to buy gold and silver coins instead of gold and silver bullion. Most Personal Articles Policies don't insure precious metals bars.

My house has a floor safe that's cemented into the ground and weighs 800 pounds (courtesy of my house's previous owner). Although floor safes are very expensive and can easily run up to a few thousand dollars, there's no way a thief can carry away my safe.

Gold and silver can also be stored in segregated storage facilities and allocated storage facilities. Both of these storage facilities are fully insured, which means that you don't have to worry about any natural disasters or robberies.

Segregated vault storage facilities allow you to store your precious metals under your own name in a secure vault. The exact gold and silver pieces that you own are put into a container, sealed, and stamped with your name and account number. When you ask to withdraw your gold or silver, the allocated storage facility will return you the exact pieces of gold and silver that you deposited. Clients legally own their precious metals, which cannot be used by the storage company in any way.

A frequently used segregated storage facility is Brinks, a world renowned security services company. Brinks is the company whose grey armored vans move cash between stores.

Allocated (aka commingled) storage facilities are different from segregated vault storage facilities in that they do not separate all the pieces of gold/silver that each client deposits. Allocated and un-segregated storage facilities merely record the amount of gold or silver that you deposited. When you withdraw your gold or silver, the storage facility gives you random pieces from their vault that are equivalent to your deposit. Allocated storage facilities charge smaller fees than segregated vault storage facilities. This is because storage companies have higher costs when they physically mark and separate all the clients' gold and silver.

You must avoid storage companies that also sell gold and silver. Some of these companies may state that your gold or silver is in a safe. In reality, they temporarily sold the gold or silver because they think that not all their clients will withdraw their gold/silver at the same time. Clients sometimes withdraw all of their gold and silver at the same time when the market price moves a lot. In these situations, the storage company won't have enough gold or silver on their hands and won't be able to satisfy their customers' withdrawal demands. This is similar to a bank run.

10. Why Silver is a Better Investment than Gold

Silver is a much better investment than gold. This is not because silver is cheaper than gold. Who cares if silver is cheaper than gold – what matters is which of these two securities yields larger profits. Just because "silver is the poor man's gold" does not mean that silver is inferior to gold. Do not let conventional "wisdom" get to your head. Silver may be the poor man's gold, but silver investors somehow end up being richer than gold investors.

Although these two assets are like Siamese twins, silver's price is much more volatile than gold's price. "Volatile" means that an asset's price fluctuates more. Silver's price fluctuates much more than gold's does. Gold's price increased 6 times from 2002 to 2011 while silver's price increased 11 times during that same period.

It is for this same reason that the Gold:Silver Ratio (more on this later) falls when gold and silver prices go up: silver's price goes up more than gold's price percentage-wise. Likewise, the Gold:Silver Ratio Ratio rises when precious metals prices fall because silver's price falls more than gold's price percentage-wise.

As an investment, we always want to buy the asset class whose price fluctuates the most. After all, the whole point of investing is to maximize our profits! As a result, silver is a much more attractive investment (or trading vehicle) than gold.

11. Add Gold and Silver to Your 401(k) or IRA

Investors using funds from their 401(k)'s can buy gold and silver ETF's or mutual funds. These investors cannot purchase physical gold or silver. This lack of choice isn't a big problem because investing in gold or silver ETF's is preferable to buying physical precious metals. In addition, investors can buy gold and silver mining stocks for their 401(k)'s, although I advise against doing so.

Gold and silver investing was approved for IRA's in 1997. For gold bullion and coins to qualify as IRA investments, they must be at least 0.995 pure. Likewise, for silver bullion and coins to qualify for IRA investments, they must be at least 0.999 pure.

Here is a list of acceptable forms of physical silver and gold that you can invest in your IRA:

1. American Gold and Silver Eagle coins.

2. Gold and silver bars.

3. Canadian Maple Leaf gold and silver coins.

4. Mexican Libertad coins.

5. Austrian Philharmonic coins.

74

6. Chinese Gold and Silver Pandas (coins).

7. Australian Kookaburra coins.

You cannot store IRA silver/gold bullion/coins yourself. These physical metals must be stored in depository institutions that are approved by the Internal Revenue Service (IRS).

After purchasing IRA silver/gold bullion/coins online, your precious metals will be shipped to your depository institution. You will receive quarterly statements for you silver or gold IRA investment account via email or mail.

12. Taxation of Gold and Silver

Various gold and silver products are taxed differently. No one wants to pay more taxes than he or she wants to. Despite paying taxes being the "patriotic thing to do", most people try to legally avoid taxes as much as they can.

Physical gold and silver bullion and coins are taxed a 28% "collectible" rate on capital gains if you own the gold or silver for more than one year. If you own gold or silver for one year or less, your investment will be taxed at the current federal and state income tax bracket. This tax structure encourages people to invest in gold and silver rather than to trade them.

Reporting purchases of physical gold and silver to the IRS is up to you, the buyer. Generally speaking, you must report any purchase of $600 or more to the IRS with a 1099 form.

Numismatic coins are taxed at the same rate as physical gold/silver bullion. However, the government generally does not collect taxes on numismatic coins. This is because too many people have rare and old coins somewhere in their attics that the government can't track down each coin.

ETF's are taxed at the normal capital gains rate of 15%. The capital gains tax applies for gold-oriented mutual funds and mining stocks as well.

As you can see, there is an additional tax disadvantage for physical gold and silver investors. Regardless of how long you own your physical precious metals, you're paying a higher tax rate than investors in precious metals financial products.

13. Good Resources for Gold and Silver Investors

The following list of resources does not include any doom-and-gloom websites or books that predict the world will end (for the 10 millionth time) or that gold and silver will go up to $1000000000000000000000000 an ounce. Let's get real here. Gold and silver are merely assets – there's nothing "magical" about them.

Jim Rogers Blog

http://jimrogers-investments.blogspot.ca/

Jim Rogers is a legendary investor who is the most successful man in the commodity (and gold/silver) markets. Jim Rogers has legendary timing – he predicts the market bottom and tops insanely accurately.

Rogers' market calls are at most a few months away from the markets' turning points.

Living in Singapore, Jim Rogers is so lonely that he frequents media outlets like CNBC to garner some attention. His interviews are generally split into 2 groups:

1 – The useless kind in which Rogers repeats what he's said for the past 12 years: commodity supplies are shrinking and demand is rising. You can practically skip over this kind of interview because there's nothing new or noteworthy.

2 – The useful kind in which Rogers explains what he thinks of the gold and silver markets right now. This is the kind of interview that you should watch. Rogers explains what he thinks gold and silver prices will do in the next year and the reasons behind his predictions.

Hot Commodities: How Anyone Can Invest Profitably in the World's Best Market by Jim Rogers

Although this book was written seven years ago, it is still somewhat relevant today. In his book Jim Rogers provides some background on the current long term bull market in commodities. Your local library probably has a copy of this book, so there's no need to buy it.

The Weekly COT Report

http://www.cftc.gov/MarketReports/CommitmentsofTraders/H
istoricalCompressed/index.htm

The U.S. Commodities Futures Trading Commission
(CFTC – a federal body) releases the Commitment of Traders
(COT) Report each Friday. This report provides a breakdown
of buying and selling volume for many commodities (gold and
silver included). Each Friday's COT report is as of that week's
Tuesday. This means that if the latest report was released on
Friday July 25, then the data reflects changes in long and short
positions as of Tuesday July 22.

You will see multiple versions of the COT Report on
the CFTC's website. Download the Excel file for the
"Disaggregated Futures-and-Options Combined Reports".
Only this report reflects TOTAL changes in long and short
positions.

There are many columns and rows in the COT excel
file. The rows represent the many different commodities. As a
gold and silver investor/trader, you only need to look at the
rows for gold and silver prices.

The columns are split into 2 groups: "total" and "changes". The "total" columns detail the total long and short positions for gold and silver. You should look at the "changes" columns. These columns show how much gold and silver are being bought or sold. The "changes" columns can be split into 2 groups. "Prod_Merc" stands for Commercial: this is the "smart money" that you should pay attention to. Commercials are the big money who professionally trade gold and silver on a large scale. "M_Money" stands for Non-commercials: this is the "dumb money". Non-commercials are the small money who trade gold and silver on a smaller scale.

Short Side of Long

http://shortsideoflong.com/

The blogger behind Short Side of Long represents the class of typical gold and silver traders. It's always interesting to see what other gold and silver traders are doing and how they view the precious metals markets' medium term outlooks.

Short Side of Long also provides some pretty good charts of the COT Report. The COT Report is merely data, so the Short Side of Long's charts help readers visualize the data. This is an example COT chart on hedge funds' silver positions as of mid-2014.

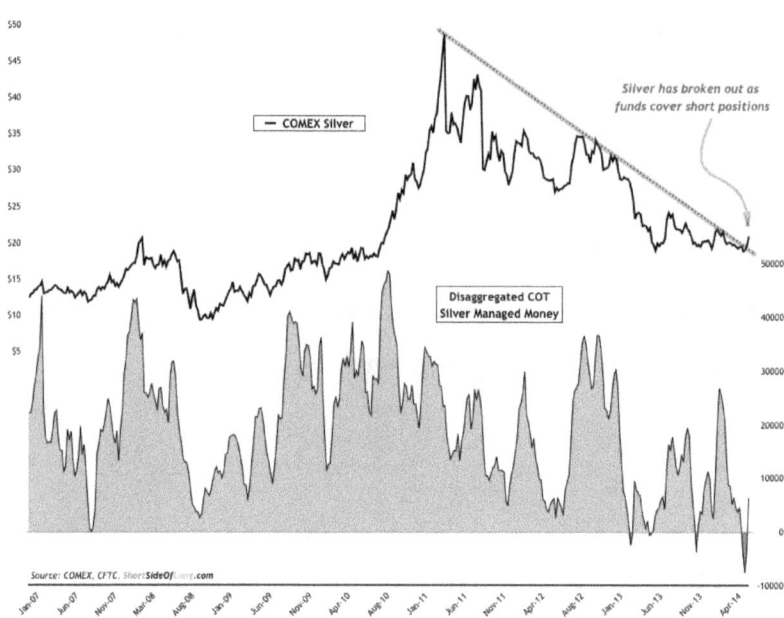

King World News: Andrew Maguire

http://kingworldnews.com/kingworldnews/Broadcast/Broadcast.html

Eric King from King World News interviews many and traders. I only listen to interviews with Andrew Maguire, a precious metals trader. Maguire is interviewed each weekend and explains his thoughts on the gold and silver markets. Andrew Maguire is by no means an excellent gold trader, or else he wouldn't be doing these interviews! Maguire represents the class of average gold traders. Listening to his interviews sheds light on what other traders are thinking and plan to do. I neither copy Maguire's trading plans nor care for his views on the precious metals markets. But by knowing how other traders view the precious metals market, I know in which direction these traders will try to push the market price in the next week. In many cases their actions become self-fulfilling prophecies in the short term.

Unfortunately, it seems like Maguire is coming on the King World News show more sporadically now. By the time you're reading this book Maguire may have stopped giving interviews.

Gold Silver Investors Club

http://www.goldsilverinvestorsclub.com/

This is actually my own (the author's) website. Each week I go over the gold and silver markets' price actions. In addition, I refresh my analysis for the long term, medium term, and short term outlook on the precious metals market.

*Note: This list is very short because there aren't many successful gold and silver investors and traders who want to publicize their exploits. All of these websites and resources provide useful data beyond the usual "doom and gloom" reports in which the whole world will end and everyone will rush to buy gold.

Part 3

Part 3 illustrates tips on how to trade gold and silver.

1. How to Develop a Gold and Silver Trading Model

Every successful trader relies on a quantified model that generates buy and sell signals. In order to successfully trade gold and silver, you must do the same. In the subsequent chapters I will show you how to build a quantified model for trading gold or silver.

Quantified models are split into 2 types: trend following models and contrarian models.

Trend following models do not predict trends in the future. Instead, trend following models try to recognize materializing trends as early as possible so that traders can jump on those trades ASAP. Trend followers don't catch the peaks or the bottoms – they catch the middle two-thirds of every trend.

Trend following works best in markets with large one-directional price movements (i.e. when prices rise or fall incessantly). This trading strategy does not work when price action is flat or whipsawing.

On the other hand, contrarian models try to predict when trends are about to reverse. This is referred to as "catching the falling knife". Contrarian traders believe that when everyone is selling, the market's bottom is almost at hand. Likewise, when everyone else is buying, the market's peak is almost at hand. Thus, contrarian traders try to buy at the bottom of a market crash and sell at the top of a bubble. To do this, contrarian models try to quantify the phrases "when everyone is buying" and "when everyone is selling".

Obviously, the problem with contrarian trading is that too many contrarian traders buy in the MIDDLE of a market crash. A contrarian model must generate a buy signal as close to the bottom of a crash as possible.

Trend following and contrarian models are built the same way. Here's how:

Step 1) Create a list of technical indicators that you want to back test. For example, my model includes sentiment, momentum, and mean-reversion indicators. Here are some of the quantified indicators that I use.

1 – Gold:Silver Ratio

2 – Fibonacci Retracements

3 – Bollinger Bands

4 – Relative Strength Index (RSI)

5 – Directional Movement Index (DMI)

Step 2) Go through a 20 year gold or silver chart and highlight all historical trades that you want your model to catch. For example, I want my gold model to generate a buy signal on November 2, 2008.

Step 3) Run each of your indicators in step 1 through all the historical trades that you highlighted in step 2. Write down the indicator value(s) for each of the historical trades. For example, RSI's (an indicator) lowest value was 18 on November 2, 2008.

Step 4) This is the tricky part. Find commonalities in the indicator values for each indicator. Look for an indicator value that allows you to enter trades at really good prices. For example, silver's price tends to bottom when it's daily RSI falls below 15.

Although these 4 steps sound simple on paper, carrying them out is very difficult. It took me over months to develop my silver model. The entire process involves a lot of back and forth trial and error.

Building a trading model isn't the same as building a rocket. There is no such thing as a model that's "complete". Trading is not a science in which there is an absolute, indisputable path that leads to success. Trading is an art in which there is no absolute right or wrong and in which there is always room for more improvement. I am always on the hunt for new indicators and better ways to build my model.

2. Indicators That I Use

The following are a few popular indicators that I use in my trading model.

The Gold:Silver ratio is commonly used by precious metals traders. To calculate the Gold:Silver ratio, just divide gold's price by silver's price. This means that if gold's price is $1200 and silver's price is $20, the ratio is 60.

The ratio determines if a price movement is valid or false. The silver market is much smaller than the gold market and silver's price moves more (percentage-wise) than gold's price. Since gold and silver prices tend to move in sync, the ratio should rise when precious metals prices fall and the ratio should fall when prices rise.

If something abnormal occurs like rising prices that are accompanied by a rising ratio, then the rise in prices is probably false and prices will cease to rise. The opposite is also true: if falling prices are coincident by a falling ratio, then the fall in prices is false and prices will cease to fall.

I use the Relative Strength Index (RSI) in my gold model. RSI is a contrarian indicator that determines when gold or silver is Oversold and Overbought. RSI does not work very well for the price of silver, but RSI's Oversold and Overbought signals work like charms for the price of gold. Looking at the following chart, you'll see that an RSI reading of 19 or less is a really good Oversold signal, meaning that the price of gold bottoms when RSI is around 19. On the other hand, an RSI reading of 78 or more is a really good Overbought signal, meaning that the price of gold peaks when RSI is around 78. You'll notice that although the RSI Overbought signal for gold is good, the RSI Oversold signal is even better.

Another indicator that I use in conjunction with RSI is Bollinger Bands (BB). Like RSI, this momentum indicator determines when gold or silver is Oversold and Overbought. Bollinger Bands are based on standard deviations. The upper Bollinger Band – the Overbought band – is based on X # of standard deviations above the price's 20 day moving average. The lower Bollinger Band – the Oversold bank – is based on X # of standard deviations below the price's 20 day moving average. If the price touches the upper Bollinger Band, the price should subsequently fall. If the price touches the lower Bollinger Band, the price should subsequently rise.

3 standard deviations tend to work best for Bollinger Bands. This is because silver's price rallies tend to peak at 3 standard deviations BB, while price declines tend to bottom at 3 standard deviations BB. Here is a chart for silver's Bollinger Bands, courtesy of Short Side of Long.

3. Risk Management

A trading model that works is only half of the equation for successful trading. The other half is a proper risk management strategy.

Trading models tell you when to buy or sell gold/silver. However, trading models cannot tell you what to do when:

A) The market price is moving against your position and your portfolio is bleeding red ink. Every model is imperfect and will inevitably generate wrong buy/sell signals. A proper risk management strategy will mitigate losses when this happens.

B) What position size to use when a trading signal is generated. Models send buy or sell signals, but they cannot tell you how much to buy or sell. With a proper risk management strategy, you can maximize your profits via position sizes while controlling your risk.

When the market price moves against your position, you need to know how to limit your losses. Too many inexperienced traders turn small losses into large losses. As

95

Warren Buffett once said, the cardinal rule to investing (and trading) is "don't lose money". If you lose 50% of your money, you'll need to make 100% just to get back to break even. There are many different ways to limit your risk.

1 – Stop losses. Stop losses are automatic orders that close your position when the market price falls below a certain level. This limits the maximum loss any trade can incur. Most traders use absolute percentage drawdowns as stop losses. Setting a stop loss at 7% below the price he paid, a trader risks no more than 7% of his capital. If the market price falls 7%, the trade disappears and the trader accepts the 7% loss. Stop losses prevent small losses from growing into big losses.

2 – Margin of safety. Margin of safety is completely different from stop loss. Traders with margin of safety on their side aren't afraid of losses. They know that if a position is losing money, the market price will eventually bounce back to the position's entry price. Thus the patient trader can exit the trade without a loss.

3 – Scale in. Scaling-in means to buy in increments. Instead of buying a full position when the price of silver or gold hits $X, you split your full position into multiple parts and buy at $X, $X-1, $X-2, $X-3… Thus, the average price of your position is

being "averaged down", and you don't need to worry about being caught in the middle of a megacrash.

Position size is very important because it heavily impacts your profits and losses. A successful trade on a tiny position (e.g. 5% of your total portfolio) yields a tiny, meaningless profit!

How you allocate position sizes depends on your trading strategy. For example, many day traders allocate miniscule 1% positions for each trade. This makes sense for them because they are trading fifteen times each day. On the other hand, a medium term trader typically risks more than 40% on each trade because he or she only trades a few times each year. In an extreme case, really good traders can risk more than 100% of their portfolio on a single trade, meaning that they leverage up.

4. Silver's Market Stages

Looking at a multi-year chart for silver prices, you'll notice that silver prices move in distinct market stages. No single silver model is universal because each of silver's market stages is very different. Silver's price action can be split into 3 distinct market stages:

1. Silver's price is steadily rising and the silver price chart looks like a mini-bubble.

2. Silver's price is steadily falling and the price chart looks like a mini-bubble that burst.

3. Silver's price action is generally flat for a long time with small waves within this consolidation phase.

Generally speaking, inexperienced traders should avoid Stage 3 in which silver trades within a long range. Silver's price will be stationary for a long time (e.g. 2 months), spike in one direction, be immobile for a long time, spike in one direction... Thus, it becomes nearly impossible to trade because:

1 – After silver experiences a long period of sideways price action, you lose confidence in your position and close it - just before the market moves.

2 – The sideways price action eliminates the usefulness of many technical indicators such as RSI & Moving Averages. Trend following indicators depend on the existence of a trend – when the price is moving sideways, no trend exists. Contrarian indicators depend upon extreme price action (either a crash or a spike in price) – when the price is moving sideways, no extremities exist.

3 – It's hard to know in which direction silver will spike.

Silver's price has been in a flat consolidation stage since the bubble burst in May 2011. If you're interested in trading silver, I suggest you stay away from it because of the dangers explained above. However, the silver bubble that burst in 2011 doesn't signal the end of the silver bull market (although that is the case with most other bull markets). The bullish fundamentals are simply so strong that they will cause another bubble (which will then be the end of the bull market).

The second bubble in silver will probably occur in 2017, the end of the bull markets for gold and silver bull. This bubble and bursting of the bubble are great for traders. By analyzing history, I've come to conclusion that all bubbles have similar characteristics. Since history repeats itself, the upcoming silver bubble will have the same characteristics.

Listed below are the 8 phases of a bubble:

1 - An insane, nearly vertical rise in price.

2 - A consolidation period that lasts typically 4 weeks.

3 - A second insane, nearly vertical rise in price.

4 - Peak

5 - Massive decline.

6 - Major correction that doesn't exceed the old high.

7 - Continuation of the bursting of the bubble.

8 - The market will usually fall 100% of the previous crazy ascent (Fibonacci retracements). When an asset starts going vertical, once the bubble bursts it will fall down to the point at which it took off.

A note of caution: don't try to predict market tops – it's impossible because mobs don't think rationally. NASDAQ in year 2000 could have ended at 3000, 5000, or 7000.

Based upon these characteristics that pervade all bubbles, it will be easy to trade the future silver bubble. Now that you know what the future price action will be like, you can easily trade accordingly.

Although you can't predict when the bubble will end, you will be ready to react quickly to because you can recognize the change in price pattern (as discussed above).

As for gold, I do not have a lot of experience trading in gold (although I do have a lot of experience investing in it). However, I've found that gold tends to be highly correlated with silver. Thus, I would trade gold just as I would trade silver. But as I've already mentioned, I'd rather trade silver than gold because silver's price moves a lot more (percentage-wise) than gold's price.

5. Gold's and Silver's Correlations to U.S. Stocks

Gold's and silver's price actions are heavily correlated to the U.S. stock market's price action. But exactly how strong is this correlation? When building my trading model, I answered three questions during three market stages: bull market, bubble, bear market.

1 – Do falling precious metals prices require falling stock prices?

2 – Do falling stock prices mean that precious metals prices will fall?

3 – Do rising precious metals prices require rising stock prices?

My conclusions are as follows.

In a bull market, precious metals prices require falling stock prices. In this same market stage, falling stock prices mean that precious metals prices will either remain unchanged or fall. In addition, rising precious metals prices require rising stock prices.

In a bubble, gold and silver's price actions are not correlated to the U.S. stock market's price action. However, the end of gold and silver's bubbles must coincide with a U.S. stock market correction.

In a bear market, precious metals prices can fall without falling stock prices. However, a medium term bounce in precious metals prices must coincide with a rise in U.S. stock prices.

The basic idea is that whenever U.S. stock prices fall more than e.g. 6%, the price of silver and gold will fall as well. This coincides with the reality that gold and silver are not safety havens in times of crisis. Gold and silver prices may spike in short term when faced by a crisis, but in the medium term gold and silver prices will fall if a crisis exists.

6. Other Correlations

Gold and silver prices are also correlated to the prices of other markets. These correlations can impact the short term price of precious metals. Thus these correlations are secondary to the precious metals – U.S. equities correlation.

Since gold and silver prices are denominated in U.S. dollars, there is a correlation between precious metals prices and the USD. A falling USD generally coincides with rising precious metals prices. The opposite is also true: a rising USD generally coincides with falling precious metals prices.

The USDX (U.S. Dollar Index) determines the value of the USD against a basket of currencies. USDX is weighted as follows:

1 – Euro: 57.6% weight

2 – Yen: 13.6% weight

3 – Pound Sterling: 11.9% weight

4 – Canadian Dollar: 9.1%

5 – Swedish Krona: 4.2% weight

6 – Swiss Franc: 3.6% weight

If USDX has reached a major support level and is very Oversold, then the USD will likely go up in the short term. Since precious metals prices are slightly correlated to the USD, precious metals prices MIGHT fall in the short term. The opposite is also true: if the USD has reached a major resistance level and is very Overbought, then the USD will likely fall and precious metals prices MIGHT rise.

As I mentioned before, gold and silver prices are correlated to other commodities' prices. The Continuous Commodity Index (CCI) is recognized as a major gauge of commodity prices. This gauge combines the three other commodity sectors – agriculture, industrial metals, and energy – with the precious metals sector to determine whether commodity prices as a whole are rising or falling. If the CCI is falling, then gold and silver prices will probably fall as well. The converse is also true: a rising CCI often coincides with rising gold and silver prices.

You should also look at other commodity sectors individually. Their correlation with precious metals works best when all three commodity sectors are moving in the same direction.

1 – Energy: the energy sector is best exemplified by crude oil. There are 2 types of crude oil: Brent Crude and WTI Crude. Although these two crude oils differ slightly in price, their price changes are almost identical percentage-wise. The most commonly traded oil ETF is USO (United States Oil Fund LP).

2 – Agriculture: the problem with agriculture is that no agricultural product can represent the entire sector. As a result, you should look at DBA (PowerShares DB Agriculture Fund), the ETF for agriculture. This ETF does a good job at tracking the agriculture sector.

3 – Industrial metals: the industrial metals sector is best exemplified by copper. The most commonly traded copper ETF is JJC.

7. Conclusion

I'm not going to bullshit you, but trading precious metals is actually a lot easier than trading U.S. equities and currencies. There is no such thing as free market capitalism anymore. The stock market and currency markets are heavily manipulated by various governments and government agencies like the Federal Reserve. You never know what politicians plan to do, which is why it's becoming more and more difficult to trade stocks.

The good thing about trading gold or silver is that these markets behave rationally. Since no governments really care about gold and silver prices, these two markets are mostly free from unnatural manipulation. Trading models work best in markets that move naturally according to the laws of capitalism.

Although gold and silver are relatively easy to trade, you still need to know what you're doing. Trading is never easy. I spent more than a year reading about trading, building my trading models, and working on my risk management strategies before I made my first trade. You cannot expect to jump into this business and shoot the lights out in the first three years. Never give up when the going gets tough, because 50% losses are normal. Never get complacent with your success, because (to quote an old and wise trader that I know) "whenever I pat myself on the back, the next feeling I get is a sharp kick down lower."

Screw the BS: How to Invest In and Trade Crude Oil

Are you interested in investing in or trading crude oil? Many aspects of the crude oil market are similar to the gold and silver markets. Check out my book on crude oil investing and trading at http://www.amazon.com/Screw-BS-Invest-Trade-Crude-ebook/dp/B00LRWCERW/

Thank you for reading Screw the BS: How to Invest in Gold and Silver. I wish you all the best in your future investment endeavors, and I will appreciate it if you leave an honest review for this book on Amazon.com http://www.screwthebs.com (this link redirects to Amazon.com)

www.ingramcontent.com/pod-product-compliance
Lightning Source LLC
Chambersburg PA
CBHW051329170526
45166CB00002B/737